DOGS AND
CATS

STEVE JENKINS

Houghton Mifflin Company   Boston 2007

For Jamie, Theo, and Jeff

Library of Congress Cataloging-in-Publication Data
Jenkins, Steve, 1952-
Dogs and cats / written and illustrated by Steve Jenkins.
    p. cm.
ISBN-13: 978-0-618-50767-2 (hardcover)
ISBN-10: 0-618-50767-1 (hardcover)
1. Dogs—Miscellanea—Juvenile literature. 2. Cats—Miscellanea—Juvenile literature. I. Title.
SF426.5.J46 2007
636.7—dc22
2006024654
Printed in Singapore

TWP 10 9 8 7 6 5 4 3 2 1

A mind of their own

Cats can be hard to understand. They act friendly and affectionate one moment, aloof and mysterious the next. Cats are the most popular pets in the world. They are also nearly perfect predators, with stealth, speed, and senses matched by no other animal. How did these fierce and independent hunters become our companions? What makes them act the way they do?

If you'd like to read about dogs, just turn the book over.

Millions of cats

All cats, large and small, are natural hunters. Wild cats must hunt to live, and they are very good at it. In fact, people first kept cats because they are such expert killers of rats, mice, and snakes. These working cats had short hair, which was less likely to get tangled or snagged in tight spaces. Later, when people began to keep cats as companions, cats with long, luxurious fur appeared.

Over the past 100 years or so, cats have been bred for more unusual features. Some have oddly shaped ears, no tail, or fur of unusual color. There are now more than forty different kinds, or breeds, of domestic cat.

All domestic cats — sometimes called housecats — are members of the same species, so any male and female cat can mate and have kittens together. They are all about the same size. Why aren't any of them really big, like some breeds of dog? One reason may be that cats have a very strong hunting instinct, and it could be dangerous for people to live with cats the size of large dogs.

Tabby

Scottish Fold

Burmese

Dogs come in more different shapes and sizes than any other mammal.

Siamese

Persian

Devon Rex

One recently developed breed of cat, the sphinx, looks as if it has no hair at all. It actually has very short, fine fur. This cat usually lives indoors, since its coat can't keep it warm. Such unusual features are called mutations. They occur from time to time in wild cats, but mutations like this don't usually help an animal survive. A nearly hairless cat in the wild would probably die before it could have kittens and pass on its mutation.

Out of Africa

The Abyssinian is one of the oldest breeds of cat. It comes from North Africa, and looks a lot like the cats in paintings found on ancient Egyptian tombs. Abyssinians have short hair and long legs, and are still popular today. Originally, people kept these cats to control pests. Cats were very valuable in ancient Egypt — some were even worshiped as gods. Killing a cat was a crime punishable by death, and taking a cat out of the country was forbidden. Eventually, though, sailors did carry off cats with them on their ships, and they spread from Africa to Asia and then to Europe. People in other parts of the world took cats into their homes, and different breeds began to develop.

The saluki is one of the oldest breeds of dog.

Except for their size, all members of the cat family are very similar — a pet cat looks and acts a lot like a lion, tiger, or leopard. This is because cats have evolved to be almost perfect hunting machines.

The wildcat

Our pet cats are directly related to the African wildcat. This fierce, solitary hunter lives in the deserts of North Africa. It is a little larger than a housecat and hunts at night, feeding on small mammals, birds, and reptiles.

Like dogs and most other predators, cats are territorial — they defend their hunting ground. A tiger's territory may cover hundreds of square miles, while a pet cat might defend just its owner's backyard.

The first catlike animals appeared around 30 million years ago. They were about the size of a modern-day domestic cat.

Follow that mouse

Cats are quiet and secretive hunters, and for most of human history they avoided people, except, perhaps, when a lion or saber-toothed cat made a meal of one of our unlucky ancestors.

For many thousands of years, humans lived by moving from place to place, hunting and collecting food. Then, about 10,000 years ago, people in Africa and the Middle East began to live in towns and villages. They planted crops and stored the grain they harvested. Soon, the stored grain attracted mice and rats, who ate much of their valuable food. These rodents, in turn, attracted the African wildcat, a stealthy and intelligent hunter that wasn't afraid to live near humans.

People found that when cats were around, there were fewer pests eating their stores of grain. At first they just let the wildcats live and hunt among their houses. Then some people began to raise cats, probably by taking kittens from their dens and caring for them. They preferred cats that were small, friendly, and good at catching mice. By 4,000 years ago, cats were living in homes and barns — they had become domesticated.

There are thirty-six different cat species living today, divided into two main groups: large cats and small cats.

The large cats include the lion, tiger, jaguar, and leopard, shown here. Large cats can roar, but small cats can't.

The lynx, shown here, as well as the domestic cat, ocelot, fishing cat, and many other species of wildcat, are all small cats. The mountain lion, which cannot roar, is also a small cat, even though it can be larger than a leopard.

I know what I like

Most cats hunt alone. This is probably one reason that people often think of cats as self-absorbed and aloof. In fact, cats can be very social. They often enjoy the company of humans and other cats.

Cats also have strong opinions about what they like and dislike. They may be choosy about where they sleep, what they eat, and whether they want to be petted or picked up. Cats let us know what they are feeling with their face, body language, voice, and scent.

Except for lions, cats in the wild don't live in groups, so, unlike dogs, they don't need a lot of ways of saying "I just want to get along." Many cat messages mean "Keep your distance." A cat that feels threatened may arch its back, fluff out its fur, and hiss. This makes it look larger and more dangerous.

Dogs are social animals and have lots of ways to express their feelings.

When a cat is happy, it holds its tail high.

When a cat rubs against a person's legs, it's not just being friendly. It is using a special scent gland on its head to leave a message for other cats that says, "This person belongs to me."

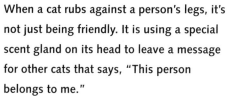

A twitching tail is a warning — best to leave this cat alone.

A purring cat with its ears facing forward and its eyes half closed is feeling content and safe.

A tail tucked close to the cat's body is a sign of insecurity.

From kitten to cat

A baby cat, or kitten, is born blind and helpless. It depends on its mother to clean it, feed it, and protect it. The kitten uses its sense of smell, which works at birth, to find its mother's milk. Kittens nurse from the same nipple every time they feed. A kitten may drink milk for eight hours a day, and sleep the rest of the time.

A group of kittens born together is called a litter. There are four or five kittens in an average litter, though some litters may include as many as twelve kittens.

Puppies are also helpless at birth.

After about a week, the kittens open their eyes. When they are about four weeks old, they begin to play with their brothers and sisters and explore their surroundings. Kittens play by stalking, leaping, and batting with their paws. They are practicing the skills they will need for hunting when they are grown. A kitten hunts instinctively — it doesn't have to be taught — but it doesn't know how to kill its prey quickly and efficiently unless the mother cat teaches it. When a cat is six months old, it may be ready to have kittens of its own. It will be full-grown by the time it is one year old.

When they are a few days old, a mother cat will often move her kittens to a new home to keep them safe from male cats or other predators. She carries them by gently grasping the scruff of their neck with her teeth. The father doesn't help — he leaves raising the kittens to the mother cat.

What's so special about a cat?

Unlike dogs, which use their endurance to run down their prey over great distances, cats are ambush hunters. They sneak up quietly or wait in hiding, then use their speed and power to leap on their prey. Almost everything about a cat — its body, its senses, its reflexes — helps it to be a more efficient and deadly hunter.

Cats cannot see color or distant detail as well as humans, but their eyes are very sensitive to movement. They are also experts at judging the distance of nearby objects. Cats can see very well in dim light.

The cat has an excellent sense of smell. It isn't quite as good as that of a dog, but it is much more sensitive than our own.

At the front of the cat's mouth are four long, sharp teeth. These are used to grab and kill prey, usually with a quick bite to the neck. The cat's other teeth are designed to tear and cut meat into chunks small enough to swallow.

Cats use their claws for hunting and climbing. They also mark their territory by scratching claw marks on trees or fences. Cats keep their razor-sharp claws hidden in a sheath until they want to use them. Combined with their powerful shoulder muscles and lightning-fast reflexes, a cat's claws are fearsome weapons.

Cats have more sensitive hearing than dogs. They can move their ears to help locate the source of sounds, and they can hear very faint and very high-pitched noises — the kind made by the rodents they hunt.

One of the most unusual features of the cat's body is its flexible spine, which allows it to perform amazing feats of balance and athleticism.

A cat's whiskers are very sensitive. With them, the cat can feel its way in the dark and can even detect temperature and wind direction.

The cat's fur keeps it warm and helps protect its skin.

The cat uses its tail for balance and to communicate with other cats.

A dog "sees" the world through its nose.

I wonder . . .

Cats have some unusual abilities, and they sometimes act in ways that don't make sense to us. Many of these actions, however, are important to a cat living in the wild. Our pet cats are just doing the things that have helped their wild ancestors survive for millions of years.

Why do cats purr?

The cat is the only animal that purrs. We are not sure exactly how cats make this sound, a soft, steady vibration. Most people know that cats purr when they are relaxed and content. A cat may also purr when it is frightened or hurt. It seems that making the purring sound is soothing and relaxing, and the cat uses its purr to help it cope with a stressful situation. Purring may also help an injured cat heal.

The strange green glow you may have seen when the headlights of a car shine into a cat's eyes at night is caused by this lining.

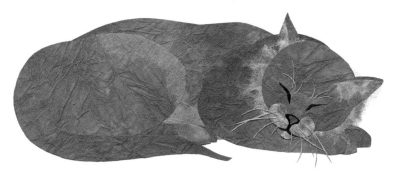

Can cats see in the dark?

A cat can see in very dim light, but not in complete darkness. Cats can see in light only one sixth as bright as that needed by a human. The cat's pupils, the black holes in the center of its eyes, can open very wide to let in light. Cats also have a special reflective lining inside their eyeballs. This lining reflects dim light back and forth, magnifying it.

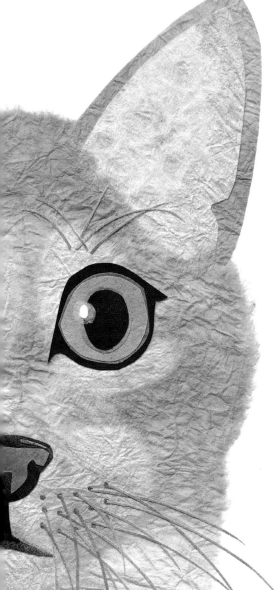

Why do cats sleep so much?

Cats sleep about sixteen hours a day, more than most other mammals (bats and sloths sleep more). Why do cats spend two thirds of their life asleep? It's probably because of the way they live in the wild. Cats need lots of rest to be able to move with the speed and power they use when hunting. A cat in the wild might also scare away much of its prey if it was awake and moving around much of the time. Our housecats still act, in many ways, like their wild relatives.

Why do cats chase their tails?

Perhaps you've seen a cat spinning around in circles, trying to grab its own tail. It looks as if the cat thinks it's chasing some other animal, but it knows quite well what it is doing. In the wild, cats spend much of their time sleeping or lying quietly. When they do move, it's often in an explosive burst of motion as they chase after and pounce on their prey. Pet cats may get their food in a bowl, but they still enjoy acting out this hunting behavior.

Do cats always land on their feet?

Please don't try this at home, but when a cat falls or is dropped upside down, it uses its balance and flexible spine to quickly turn right-side up and land on its feet. A cat can actually be hurt more seriously by falling just a short distance, because it may not have time to flip over. If it falls from a great height, such as a ten-story building, it relaxes in the air and spreads out its legs to slow its fall. Though cats can be hurt or killed in a tumble like this, many have walked away from falls that few other animals could survive.

Why do dogs bury bones?

Why do cats scratch the furniture?

Not all cats do this. Some scratch trees, or are trained to use a special scratching post. But unless their claws have been removed — a bad thing to do to a cat — all cats scratch. They do this to remove the old, dull sheath that covers their claws, keeping them razor sharp. Cats may also leave scratch marks as a message to other cats, saying, "This is my territory."

Are cats smarter than dogs?

It depends on what we mean by "smart." Unlike dogs, cats usually do only what they want to do. Dogs evolved as a member of a social group, and may have more ways to express themselves. They can also understand and follow more commands than a cat. Many cat owners, however, believe that a cat's independence, sensitivity to its surroundings, and impressive abilities as a hunter mean that it is smarter than a dog.

Amazing cat facts

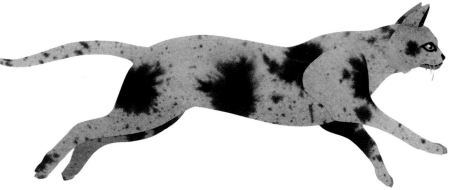

A cat can run as fast as 31 miles per hour (50 kilometers per hour).

Cats do not have a collarbone, so they can fit their bodies through a very small opening — anything bigger than their head.

The world's fattest cat was a male tabby that weighed more than 46 pounds (21 kilograms).

The average cat weighs about 10 pounds (4½ kilograms).

A female cat can have a litter of kittens every four months. We know of one cat that gave birth to 420 kittens over her lifetime.

A cat's tongue is covered with tiny backwards-pointing barbs that scoop up water as the cat drinks. It can also use its rough tongue to groom itself and scrape meat from bones.

Cats spend about one third of their waking time grooming themselves by licking their fur with their tongue. Most people that are allergic to cats are actually allergic to the dried saliva on their fur.

All kittens are born with blue eyes.

An average cat eats the equivalent of 5 mice a day.

Cats cannot taste sweets, and do not like to eat them.

In the Middle Ages, superstitious people thought cats were connected with witches and the devil, and many cats were killed. Cats became popular again when the Black Plague swept through Europe in the 1500s, killing millions of people. The disease was spread by flea-carrying rats, and people realized that cats could help reduce the number of rats.

Cats often bring their owners gifts of dead mice and birds, sometimes placing them neatly on a pillow or table.

There are many formulas for calculating the age of a cat in human years. Here is one:

First cat year = 16 human years

Second cat year = 7 human years

Each cat year after that = 4 human years

So, a 4-year-old cat would be (16 + 7 + 4 + 4) or 31 human years old.

Cats live an average of 16 years, or 79 in human years.

The world's oldest cat, Granpa, lived 34 years and 2 months. Using our formula, this would make him 151 years old. Do you think he was named Granpa as a kitten?

Cats were mummified in ancient Egypt, and mice were placed with them in their tombs. More than 300,000 mummified cats were found in one Egyptian cat cemetery.

Some cats can jump seven times their own height. An adult human who could do this would be able to leap to the top of a three-story building.

The Newfoundland has webbed feet.

Cats with blue eyes and white fur are usually deaf. White-furred cats can also get sunburned.

There are more than 500 million domestic cats in the world — more than any other pet. This compares to about 400 million dogs.

Friends or enemies?

Cats and dogs in the wild do not get along well — they are natural enemies, competing for a limited food supply. As pets, however, they often live together in the same house. They may ignore each other, or they may play together like the best of friends.

If you'd like to read about dogs, just turn the book over and start from the other side.

Friends or enemies?

Dogs and cats in the wild do not get along well — they are natural enemies, competing for a limited food supply. As pets, however, they often live together in the same house. They may ignore each other, or they may play together like the best of friends.

If you'd like to read about cats, just turn the book over and start from the other side.

Most dogs are friendly and gentle, but a few bite. Every year, thousands of people are seriously hurt when they are bitten by a dog, and a few people are killed. No one should try to pet a strange dog without first asking its owner if it is friendly. Even then, one should approach the dog gently, without making sudden movements or loud sounds that might frighten it.

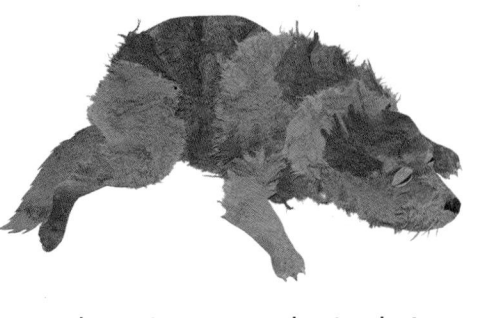

Dogs dream. Sometimes a sleeping dog's eyes will move, its feet will twitch, and it may whine or bark. No one knows what dogs dream about.

The average dog lives 14 years, and small dogs usually live longer than large ones. There are many ways to calculate a dog's age in human years. Here is one simple formula:

First dog year = 15 human years

Second dog year = 9 human years

Each dog year after that = 4 human years

So, a 4-year-old dog would be (15 + 9 + 4 + 4), or about 32 human years old.

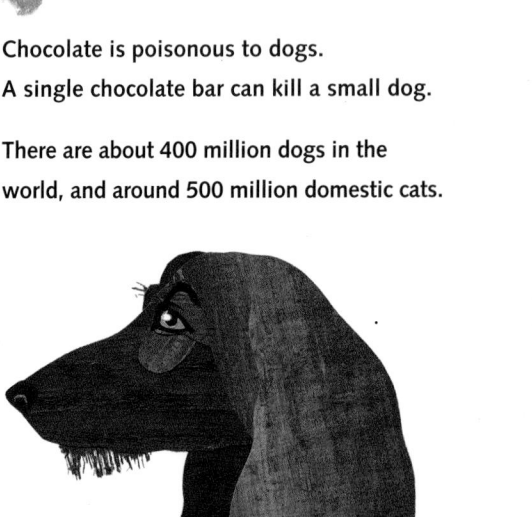

The oldest dog we know of was an Australian cattle dog named Bluey. He lived 29 years and 5 months. This would have made him almost 134 years old in human years.

The Newfoundland, a large dog bred to fetch fishermen's nets and rescue drowning sailors, has webbed feet. A few Newfoundlands still work as official lifeguards in England, Italy, and the United States.

Chocolate is poisonous to dogs. A single chocolate bar can kill a small dog.

There are about 400 million dogs in the world, and around 500 million domestic cats.

Finding out how quickly a dog can learn from experience is one way of measuring its intelligence. For example, a dog might get a reward by fetching a ball whenever a bell rings. How many times must this sequence be repeated before the dog understands what to do? Based on tests like this, some of the smartest dogs are the border collie, poodle, German shepherd, and golden retriever. Most experts agree that the dumbest dog is the Afghan hound.

Border Collie

Afghan Hound

Amazing dog facts

The Saint Bernard is, on average, the heaviest breed of dog. A big Saint Bernard weighs as much as 200 pounds.

The smallest dog breed, on average, is the Chihuahua. It stands only 7 inches (18 centimeters) tall. Chihuahuas also live longer than any other breed — 18 years or longer.

The record for the world's smallest dog, however, is held by a Yorkshire terrier less than five inches (12 centimeters) tall.

The largest dog we know of was an English mastiff named Hercules, who weighed 282 pounds (128 kilograms).

A Russian dog named Laika was the first living being in space. Laika was aboard a satellite launched in 1957. There was no way to get her back to earth, and she died in her space capsule.

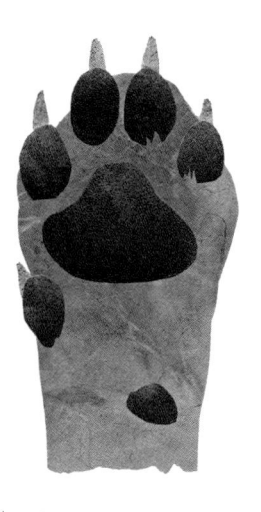

Unlike people, dogs can't sweat through their skin — an overheated dog cools itself off by panting and by sweating through the pads of its feet.

In ancient China, people carried tiny dogs in the sleeves of their gowns to help keep their hands warm.

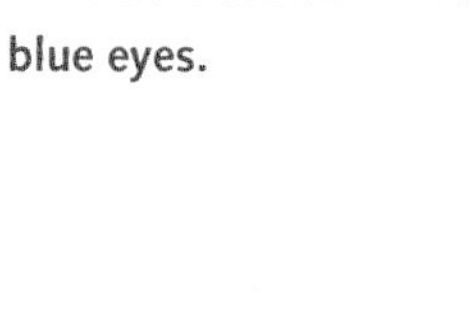

All kittens are born with blue eyes.

Why do cats sleep so much?

Why do dogs bury bones?

When wild dogs kill a large animal, they eat as much of it as they can at one time. If they leave any of their kill uneaten, other animals will finish the job. So the dogs bury pieces of meat to dig up and eat later. When a dog buries a bone in the backyard, it is imitating its wild relatives.

Why do dogs eat grass?

We aren't really sure why dogs do this. They may like the taste, or might just want something to chew on. It's possible that dogs eat grass to settle their stomach or to help them throw up food that is making them feel bad. Wild dogs often eat the stomachs of the grazing animals they hunt. Since these animals frequently have a belly full of grass, plants are a normal part of a wild dog's diet.

Are dogs smarter than cats?

It depends on what we mean by "smart." Dogs evolved as social animals, and they are better than cats at communicating with people. They can understand more words and gestures than cats and are good at learning how to do new things. These abilities make many dog owners believe that dogs are smarter than cats.

I wonder . . .

Dogs sometimes do things that seem odd to us. Many of these behaviors are left over from a time before dogs separated from wolves. They are instinctive — dogs are born knowing how to do them. Strange as some of these things seem to us, they make sense if we understand how they helped our dogs' wild ancestors survive.

Why do dogs bark at strangers?
When dogs bark at people or other dogs that they do not know, they are protecting their territory. They are saying, "This space is mine — stay away." This protective instinct is one of the main reasons that people first wanted dogs around.

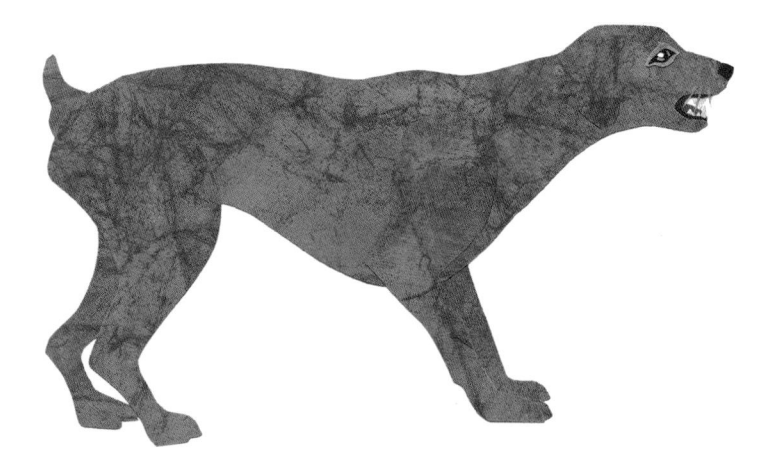

Why do dogs chase balls?
Few dogs can resist running after a thrown ball. A dog's eyes are very sensitive to movement. When a dog sees a moving ball, its hunting instinct takes over and off it goes, the way a wild dog chases a small animal. This chasing instinct is why it's not a good idea to try to run away from an aggressive dog.

Why are dogs easy to housebreak?
A housebroken dog is one that knows it should not go to the bathroom in the house. Instead, it will try to go outdoors. Puppies have to be taught where to go, but they have an instinctive sense that they should not soil their home. This is because dogs evolved as den animals, living in caves or burrows. Their dens would become dirty and unhealthy if they relieved themselves inside.

Why do dogs roll in manure?
Given the chance, many dogs will roll in horse or cow manure. This can be very unpleasant for their owners, but it makes sense to the dogs. When hunting, a wild dog will roll in the dung of grazing animals to hide its own scent, allowing it to sneak up on its prey.

Dogs have very sensitive hearing. They can hear sounds that are much too faint or high-pitched for us to notice.

Dogs have strong bones and muscles, and a thick coat that protects their skin and keeps them warm.

A dog uses its tail for balance and to express its feelings.

Dogs walk on their toes, not on the soles of their feet. Each foot has four tough pads that act as shock absorbers and help the dog grip the ground.

Some of a cat's senses are even sharper than a dog's.

What's so special about a dog?

Unlike cats, which use explosive speed and power to catch their prey, dogs are endurance hunters. Wild dogs can run for miles, pursuing an animal until it stops from exhaustion. Their bodies and senses help them find and catch prey. They also help the dog keep track of and communicate with other members of its pack.

Dogs are not color blind, but they don't see color or detail as well as we do. However, they are much better at detecting movement, and they have sensitive night vision — important abilities for a hunter.

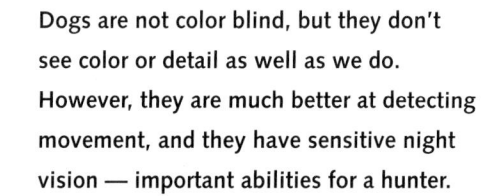

The dog's most important sense is its powerful sense of smell. It's hard for us to imagine, but a dog "sees" the world through its nose. Dogs can detect odors that are thousands — perhaps even millions — of times too faint for us to smell. Dogs use their sense of smell to hunt, to find their way around, and to interpret messages from other dogs.

Dogs have sharp front teeth for grasping and killing prey, as well as strong, scissorlike back teeth for cutting meat into chunks and gnawing on bones. Dogs are meat eaters, but they will also eat fruit, nuts, and other plant foods.

The dog's sense of taste is not as good as ours, but its sense of smell makes up for this.

Whiskers are very sensitive, and tell a dog a lot about its surroundings. A dog running through thick brush will close its eyes to protect them whenever its whiskers touch something.

When it is about four weeks old, a puppy begins to take an interest in the world around it and play with its brothers and sisters. Play is important — it is the way a dog learns how to hunt, and how to get along with other dogs and people.

By the time it is one year old, a dog is full-grown and can have puppies of its own.

Kittens, like puppies, are blind and helpless at birth.

From puppy to dog

A dog begins its life as a puppy — a tiny, furry creature that is almost completely helpless. Its eyes are closed and its ears are sealed. The puppy's nose, however, works as soon as it is born, and the newborn dog uses it to find its first meal — its mother's milk.

A group of puppies born together is called a litter. An average litter is six or seven pups, but it may be as small as one puppy or as large as twenty. The mother dog takes good care of her puppies during the first few months of their lives, feeding, protecting, and teaching them. The father doesn't have much to do with raising the pups, but he may give them a lesson by nipping or growling at them if they play too roughly.

When a puppy is one or two weeks old its eyes and ears open. Soon it needs solid food, which the mother provides by throwing up some of the food she has eaten. For the first few weeks of its life, a puppy doesn't do much except sleep and eat.

Dogs express many of their feelings with their voice. They whine, whimper, snarl, howl, yip, and bark. A bark can be excited, happy, or angry.

Many of a cat's messages mean "Please leave me alone."

Who's the boss?

Dogs, like wolves, are social animals. A dog always wants to know its place in the pack. When two dogs meet, they try to figure out which dog is dominant. This isn't always the biggest or toughest dog. A big dog will often submit to a small, aggressive dog, especially if they meet on the small dog's territory.

One of the main reasons that dogs get along so well with humans is that they naturally want to be part of a group. Pet dogs think of the people they live with as their pack. It's important to let a dog know that a human is its pack leader. A dog that thinks it is in charge can be troublesome — even dangerous.

Dogs express their feelings in many ways. They communicate with us — and with other dogs — by using their voice, face, body language, and scent. Paying attention to these things can help us understand what a dog is feeling.

A happy or excited dog wags its tail, holds its head up, and opens its mouth. Sometimes it will also stand up on its back legs.

When a dog crouches low with its back end in the air and its tail wagging, it is saying, "I want to play."

This dog stands tall, holds its head high, puts up its ears, and curls its lip, saying, "I'm in charge here."

Crouching down with its tail tucked between its legs, its ears laid back, and its mouth closed, this dog is saying, "You're the boss — I don't want to fight."

Where did the first dogs come from?

Dogs have been living with people for at least 14,000 years, and perhaps much longer. The first modern humans — people like us — lived in Africa more than 100,000 years ago. Wolves were probably attracted to the animal scraps and leftovers that these people threw out. Some wolves weren't afraid to live near people, and they found that it was easier to eat scraps than to hunt and kill their own prey. The humans' camp became the territory of these wolves, and they helped defend it from other wild animals. People realized that having wolves around was a good thing. For thousands of years, the wolves remained wild animals, living on the outskirts of human settlements. At some point, however, people probably took wolf pups from their dens and raised them. Wolves that were too aggressive were killed or driven off, so the tamer wolves were most likely to survive and have pups of their own. After thousands of generations, these animals were no longer wild wolves — they had become dogs.

Our pet cats are all related to the fierce African wildcat.

Coyote

Bush Dog

Fennec Fox

Dogs have many wild relatives, including the jackal, the coyote, the South American bush dog, wolves, and twenty kinds of foxes.

Wolves, dogs, cats, bears, and weasels — in fact, all meat-eating mammals that live on land — are the descendants of a small tree-dwelling mammal called Miacis that lived about 55 million years ago.

Plays well with others

All dogs are the descendants of the gray wolf, a swift and powerful hunter. Wolves have tough bodies, excellent vision and hearing, an amazingly good sense of smell, and strong, sharp teeth. They live together in groups called packs. A wolf is about the same size as a large dog, but by working together in a pack, wolves can catch and kill animals as big as a moose. The members of a pack must communicate with one another to raise pups, choose mates, hunt, and avoid fights. Each pack has a dominant wolf — a leader — and a set of rules that all pack members follow.

Like most hunting animals, wolves are territorial. Each pack lives and hunts in a large area that it defends against predators, including other wolf packs.

favored. After many years a new breed of dog — the saluki — had been created.

In the same way, over many generations, dogs that were used to herd livestock, guard houses, kill rodents, or do other kinds of work gradually took on the size and shape best suited to their jobs.

No matter the breed, all dogs are members of the same species. This means that any male and female dog can mate and have puppies, no matter how different they look. By carefully selecting the mother and father, dog breeders can "design" a dog. They choose parents of a particular size, color, or personality to mate and produce pups with new features.

The first domestic cats were kept to kill mice and rats.

When dog breeders try to create unusual-looking dogs or exaggerate a breed's features, they can create dogs with serious health problems. The bulldog, for instance, often has trouble breathing and walking.

Most of the world's dogs are not pure breeds. They are mixtures of several different kinds of dog — what some people call mutts. Mixed-breed dogs are often smart, healthy, and even-tempered, and many dog owners prefer them.

How is a dog breed created?

The saluki is one of the oldest dog breeds. It is a sight hound — a fast, long-legged dog that hunts with its eyes instead of its nose. Six thousand years ago, people hunted game with sight hounds on the open plains of the Middle East.

How did these early hunters create a saluki? Well, they didn't start out with a particular kind of dog in mind. People took dogs along on their hunts and saw that some were better than others at spotting and catching game. Dogs with long legs and good eyesight were the best hunters. People took good care of these valuable dogs, so they were more likely to survive and have pups of their own. With each new generation, the fastest dogs with the sharpest vision were

In a three-mile race, the saluki is the fastest mammal on earth.

Big dogs, little dogs . . .

Dogs come in more shapes and sizes, or breeds, than any other mammal. The first dog breeds looked a lot like wolves, their close relatives. These early dogs helped guard people's homes and villages. Over time, as people used dogs to herd livestock, hunt, and pull sleds, different breeds of dog developed. Not all dogs had to work. Some were raised to be companions for people.

Nowadays, many dogs are bred for the way they look. They may be very large or very small, or have coats of unusual length, color, or pattern. A few have exaggerated features, like the flat face of the pug or the long, low body of the dachshund.

Altogether, there are more than 400 breeds of dog. Some are still working dogs. They guide blind people, rescue victims of earthquakes and avalanches, and help the police. Others find game for hunters, or herd sheep and cattle. Most dogs today, however, are pets.

Mexican Hairless   **Briard**   **Shar-Pei**   **Miniature Pinscher**   **Dachshund**

Domestic cats are all about the same size.

Pug

Great Dane

Border Collie

Man's best friend?

Why do dogs and people get along so well? Are dogs really our loyal, understanding friends? Dogs have lived with people for thousands of years and were the first animals to be domesticated, but they are also natural predators. Dogs have strong bodies, sharp teeth, and keen senses. How did we end up sharing our homes with animals that were once fierce wild hunters?

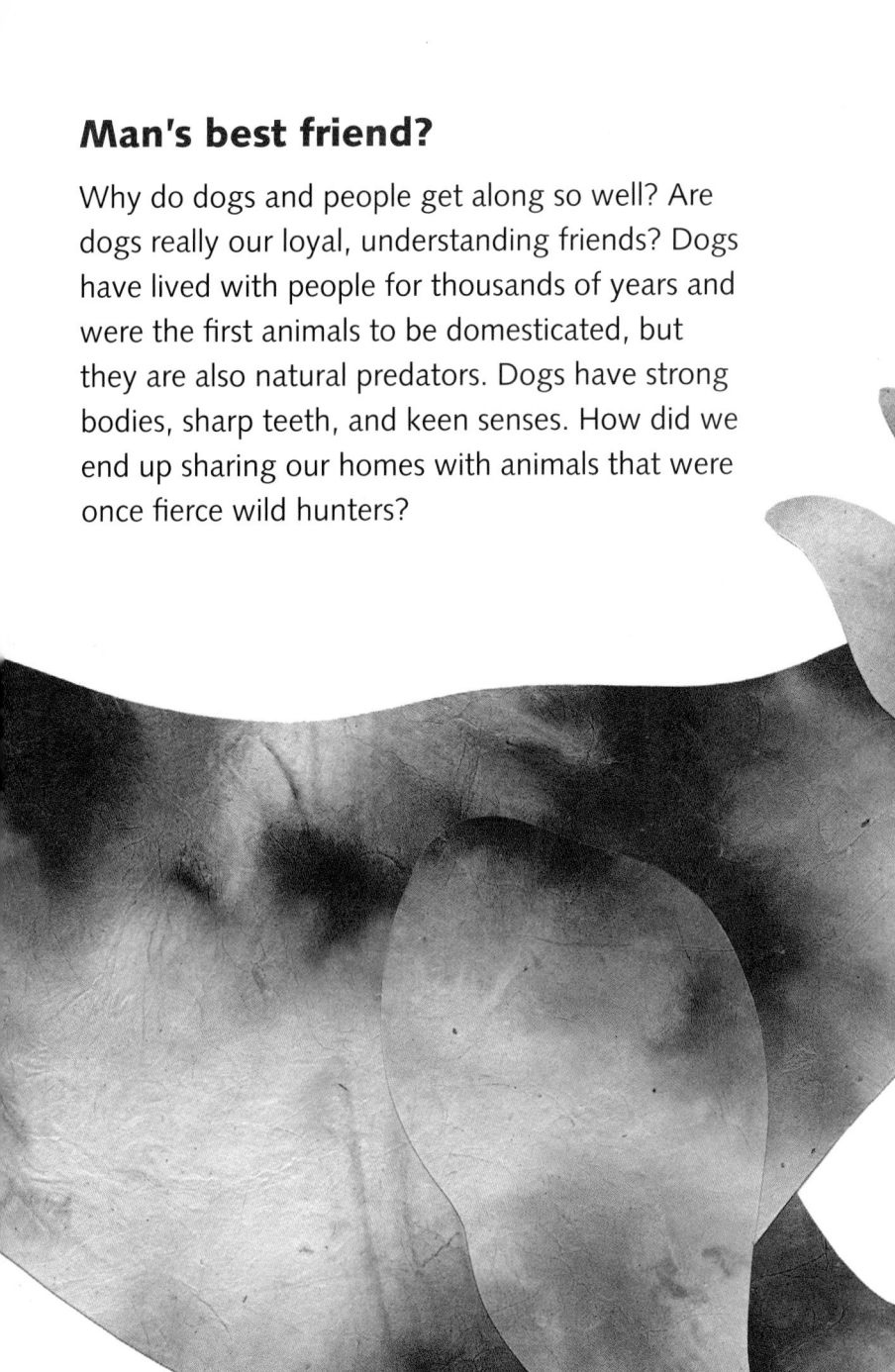

If you'd like to read about cats, just turn the book over and start from the other side.

For Jamie, Jeff, and Theo

The illustrations in this book are cut and torn
paper collage. Many of the papers were made by
hand. They come from Egypt, France, India, Italy,
Japan, Mexico, Nepal, Thailand, the Philippines,
and the United States.

The text is set in Syntax Roman and bold.

STEVE JENKINS

DOGS
AND CATS

Houghton Mifflin Company   Boston 2007